CHOSEN

ISAIAH VAN

Paperback: 978-1-961438-81-1
eBook: 978-1-961438-82-8
Library of Congress Control Number: 2023916645

Ordering Information:

Prime Seven Media
518 Landmann St.
Tomah City, WI 54660

Printed in the United States of America

Table of Contents

Introduction

*A*s a child I was always trying to find my place in the world, either by defining myself to a cause or someone else desperately attempting to fit in as everyone constantly told me that it was important to always love myself, something that was not necessarily registering with me. I'm someone that always wanted to make an impact in the world, to make the impossible possible. Many individuals just simply believed that some things could not be explained but I always believed there was an answer because even in our darkest days there is always that spark of light willing you to do better, to be better. I have experienced many losses and I have had many wins. As a child I always had a fear of leaving the house because I felt like the world was so big and I felt so connected to everyone and everything in it but lived in fear that the world would was so dangerous. There are drugs killing people, murders, rape, the risk of someone not liking someone simply because they made a choice that was for the good of themselves. It frightened me thinking there was not enough love and compassion in the world, and I knew that if I got caught up in that I would lose myself. We are not always responsible for the fact that other people have darkness in them but what do you do when y ou feel like their pain is now your pain too? We make choices that send us down certain paths but isnt there anyone else out there in the world that knows what feels like this? Like a huigher power keeps calling out to me but you were unwilling to listen because of your ego getting in the way, mostly because you had to put up walls to protect yourself from getting hurt ever again. You love everyone and have compassion for all of them, but they do not always feel the same. Of course they are in pain and it is hard trying to shine your light and the darkness continuously tries to dim it and at a point you let the darkness in because you start to feel like the world will never understand why you do care and act the way you do because all you ever wanted was peace and once you start to feel like that is just impossible to have it you let it in more but it never completely takes you over as there is a part of the light it could never touch Sometimes when the whole world is trying to turn you into something that you're not and you still find a way to keep on going, that is what it truly means to be a warrior. We are all on separate journeys but in some ways, we are all connected as well. Many of us have love for one another but I believe love is most powerful, most magical when you can give it to yourself first. We are all here to live a life of freedom and although I Invision a society where we can all be peaceful with one another that is just not going to always be the case as some conditioning may be hard to break when it comes to constantly attempting to walk a mile in someone else's shoes other than our own. We can either allow our traumas to constantly have a hold over us our entire life or we can break free of that prison and rise to the person we were always destined to be. We all have gifts that need to be expressed in the world and yes there are some that are more gifted than oth ers, but we are all uniquely made. It is not easy falling in love with yourself after you were conditioned to feel l like you were the complete opposite, but I have come to a place to respect and honor the man I am still becoming. Friends and family and even co-workers have told me how beautiful of a man I am and how intelligent I am. As a child I always found myself drawn to certain people or loved watching certain tv shows or movies, and they all had to do with chosen ones as I always found myself drawn to them. My mom and siblings would often remind me that I lived in fantasy land all the time. I have always also been a believer in fairy tales as well and magic, constantly attracted to the paranormal. Many of my friends and family would also say that I'm an extremely sensitive person or crazy. I never thought too much into it, but I did realize as I was getting more and more older, I became more sensitive and was told I was weird even more. At one point life took a dark turn which led to a shocking revelation about myself that changed my life forever. Everyone has a beginning, middle and an end and this is where my journey of self-discovery begins.

CHAPTER 1
Childhood

The year was 1994, and my mom and mom were living in a small town in Pennsylvania with my little brother Andre and my grandmother Jackie who was paralyzed in a hospital bed while my older brother Ronald was in prison due to drug dealing. Mom tried to do the best she could taking care of me and my little brother, but these were not easy tasks. I always felt closer to mom as we did just about everything together. There is was an instance when my mom and I went shopping along with my godmother and godbrother and we were waiting for the bus. Mom realized that she wanted to go back and quickly grab something assuming she would have time to make it back before the bus showed up. My anxiety started to take over as I started to get this intense feeling of worry that she was not going to make It back on time. It was almost like I could see it in my head playing out like a movie and me screaming in tears because she was going to miss the bus. I could never take it being separated from my mother as she was the person I adored most in the world. Just as I saw it in my mind, the bus showed up and mom still was not back yet. There were several attempts that were tried by myself to try to run back and get here even if I did miss the bus but my god brother as well as God mother were pulling me back and made me get on to the bus. I wanted to punch the bus window in or kick it, anything that I could to get off the bus to reunite with my mother, the women I have much in common with, the woman I feel most at piece when I am around. We have had a bond that is like no other. It is a terrible feeling when you feel like you are being taken away from your parents because you feel like you may never see them again and that is exactly how I began to feel. I was kicking and screaming on the bus as my god mother and God brother were holding me back as I was attempting to go after my mom. When I arrived at home, I was certainly in for shock, as mom had already beaten us there. I was too young to know about cabs and taxis and that is of course what she had taken home. The feeling of relief took over because I had the one person that meant so much to me back. People are always telling me that I over analyze or over think and sometimes that is used to my benefit. Me and my younger brother did not know much about dad except for the fact that he was in prison and that he would be out soon. Prison has always been something that frightened me, being stuck in that tight space like a caged animal just seems unbearable, especially for someone like me who has had asthma his own life. Andre was always too busy looking in the mirror trying to be the pretty boy to impress the girls. Andre and I were always getting ourselves into trouble. Everyone always looked to me as the responsible one with a rebellious side. My older brother wrote letters every chance he could get about how he was going to do better, and he loved us all but there were times when it was not always easy to escape his past. The road to happily ever after can be very bumpy but achievable. Me and my little brother Andre were not always with mom as she had some secrets of her own. We did not always notice it and there is the fact that we were too young to understand but mom had a drug problem. Andre did not really understand what was happening with mom, he was always active as he was always out playing with his friends or sleeping over another friend's home, or you know he was with me getting into some kind of trouble unaware of what was happening with mom. I always knew something was not right as i always had a deep sense of something either not being right in life or I dedicated myself to fixing someone else's problem, I was a problem solver. Sometimes my ambition when it comes to solving things would also end up landing me in trouble. I have always been incredibly misunderstood to the point where I did not quite understand myself either, which turned out to be something greater than I ever could have imagined but more on that later. As for mom and her drug problem, one thing I can always say is that my mom loved me and my two brothers with every bit of her soul as she made sacrifice after sacrifice for us even if it took away her happiness a little bit. Every single day I would always look into mom's eyes, and it was either pain I felt, or I felt her need to make sure we were all happy. Now when you're trying to make sure your kids are happy every day, as well as the boyfriend who helped raise me and Andre can be quite a lot to handle. Mom did a lot for so many, especially her family. She reminded me a lot of Supergirl, always trying to save the world but times were not always so good, she may have found her way to sobriety, to the lord and to the light.

CHAPTER 2

Foster Care and back to mom

My mother had a history with drugs and that caused many issues which led to me, and my brother being taken into foster care, and I could never hate her because she is the very best friend I could ever ask for. Mom always had such an amazing heart with so much compassion and empathy for others and she was truly a gift to this world. She was a warrior that like me endured so much from others just for being the loving person she is. Mom always took accountability for her actions. She was the biggest inspiration in my life. Mom passed away in 2014 but she is always with me. It is only goodbye for now, we will see each other again but until then not only am I going to make myself proud but I am going to make you proud as well and to this day can hear her voice in my head " Isaiah all that I want is for you to live a happy, liberating life, that is what will make me happy. As a child so many weird occurrences would happen that I just could never forget. I had one dream where I was walking in this park at night and in the dream, I felt so much darkness around me like something just was not right. It felt so cold in the dream, and it was always the same thing I kept seeing over and over in my head like I was watching a movie but the images that I kept seeing in my head played a lot faster than in the movies. Those images that were playing in my head would soon become a reality later in my life. I have always had the occurrences happening to me as a child that I could not make sense of. I am someone that loves to look up in the sky but sometimes I wonder if others sensed that there was something up there whether that would be aliens are something else. I would say to myself, can't you guys feel it? Sometimes I feel like I am a part of the universe in a way that I cannot even explain. I certainly feel connected to God, the creator of the universe in such an incredible heavenly way. Nobody is perfect, that is something that is overrated, and my dad was far from perfect but his love for me and my brothers has surely been felt even when he made some mistakes of his own that landed him in prison. My dad sent letters every single chance he got and there were a countless number of times I imagined what it would be like if mom and dad got back together. I'm sure there are many kids and even young teens that have wished mom in dad could get back together. My grandmother had some health issues, so we went back and forth between two cities. We had a small apartment but it was always lovely seeing my grandmother. I loved to sneak under her bed and sneak her snacks why she was always sleeping or well at least so I thought. I could hear her to this day" boy!!! You better not be in my snacks" I guess I was not quick enough. There were even times when I would be in the kitchen, and she would still somehow knew. It was almost like mom mom which is what we called our grandmother was psychic or something. Me being someone that believes in it always felt connected to the earth in a way that I could never really explain. I never felt like I clicked with anyone really. I certainly never liked being in social crowds. There were times when I really wanted to be outside and there were times when I wanted to stay in mostly because I wanted to watch my tv shows in movies but also because i felt like the world was too big, so I had to hide from it and yes i did have a fear of failure. My mom did not care much if I stayed in because all she wanted was for me to be happy. She was a earth angel in the truest sense and she was always my biggest inspiration to this day. Me and my younger brother never really understood why mom acted a certain way sometimes, little did we know it was because she was high on drugs every other day. No matter what my love for her never changed as she is my entire world. Me and my mother were alike in many ways and everything that I ever did in my life I wanted to do with her whether that would be watch a lifetime movie or a horror movie and our soap operas together. She loved to watch her soap operas every day at noon. I have been watching soap operas for as long as I can remember. It is nice to escape our own world for just a while and soaps are a good way to do so. Me and mom loved to go out and eat and eat in restaurants together.

CHAPTER 3

Am I clairvoyant? And Dad returns

*M*om's boyfriend would go out to eat with us, but I was more than happy when he did not come. Victor was his name and I never really liked him, there was always this bad feeling I got that he would leave her one day when she needed him the most, especially when it came to her health. People always told me that I seem to be really good at picking up on certain things, but I never thought too much of it just like when I had bizarre dreams like I was connected to the weather. One dream that was constant that I always saw was a dream about a storm coming that was going to be big like world changing big. I kept seeing the same thing over and over in my head to the point it felt so real like some of my other dreams. There was also this feeling I kept getting that something big was going to impact my life. The older I got, the closer I felt it coming and I knew it was going to be bad, but I also knew it would lead to something greater. The same thoughts were roaming in my head" What is happening to me? If I talk about it is someone going to think that I am crazy? The storm that I felt coming I could feel more and more, and it scared me very much. Could this dream about the coming storm have to do with what would become of my life or could it have to do with the pandemic that would begin in 2020. It is my theory that it could have had to do with both. Dreams can certainly mean more than one specific thing. Most people would probably say something is wrong with me which some say to this present day. Even though my mom and her boyfriend were on again off again I hoped that my mom and dad would one day give it another shot. The year was 1996 and dad was being released from prison and I remember being extremely nervous to see him because i was so young when he left so it felt like I was getting to know him all over again as me and my younger brother did not remember much about him, but my older brother remembered more. When dad visited while me and my younger brother were living with my grandmother as mom was taking care of her I just wanted to say mom and dad together in the same sentence like you see on tv with the children saying mom and dad in the same sentence. My dad has always been so protective of us and my older was always the same in an incredibly irritating way, but it was all love, so I understand. I am the one that is more like my mom personality wise, and my younger brother has always looked like my mom. Me and my older brother looked more like my father, but my older brother was more like him as far as his personality. When dad came to visit, he talked about some of the ups and downs that they faced in their relationship as I wanted to know more about their history together.

CHAPTER 4

High school and more Bullies and discovering more about my sexuality

*Y*ears passed and from elementary school all the way up until I started high school, I had been bullied. I had hoped that it would be different in high school but that was not the case. I was beginning my soap more year at high school. My younger brother was either in school or off camp during the summer and my older brother was home from prison and was in a relationship that had its obstacles that is for sure. His girlfriend was expecting, and I always said that if she ever did get pregnant that it would be a girl and sure enough, she did end up having a girl so apparently, I got that prediction right. Mom's boyfriend was away for work a lot, so it was always just us there at home watching a lot of lifetime movies and soaps operas which was fantastic and fun. One night while mom and I were watching a movie she said to me that she was feeling off and she began to shake intensely and hit the floor as I watched in horror. I immediately called 911 in an intense panic and in tears as mom was sitting there unconscious and they told me to do a few things until they arrived, and I did. All I have ever wanted to do is make sure she is safe from any negativity, any type of drama. I made it my mission to protect mom from all of that. I did not care who disliked me. If I had to fight or argue with my siblings to make sure that she was happy then that is what I would do. I always knew that I liked guys instead of girls so that was never up for debate but the older I was getting I was becoming more and more curious about experimenting so I would go into chat rooms on the family computer and plan on meeting on meeting up with someone which is a dangerous move but i become tired of not getting the chance to explore that side of myself. I was never open about my sexuality with my parents and siblings, not like how I was with my friends. There were occasions my older sibling and I would argue, and fight and he would call me many names and d I would just scream and shout at him so "So what!!!! Yes, I am!!!! I know brothers and sister fight so the next day we just pretended like nothing happened. Mom 's on again off again boyfriend Ronald and I would even get into these arguments where he would also call me out about my sexuality. I guess sometimes I did not make that clear, but I have learned to not dwell on the past and just live in the present and simply go with the flow. Something I could never forget is the time mom went into my room and found something that was inappropriate for my age. She was so upset about it, that she went to call my father. I could feel mom's pain very deeply like she felt like I turned out the way I did because she did something wrong, the same that I felt from her, and the embarrassment was also heavily felt. As dad and I were talking on the phone as he was yelling at me asking me if I was gay. The words could not come out of my mouth correctly, so I froze up until he moved on to the next subject. It was all becoming so much as I have been called so many names by so many, it was either I am ugly, a pathetic queer, stupid, retarted,looser and just about every name in the alphabet that was mean. Mom always suspected that I was gay, and dad even suspected that I was gay going as far as to tell me to stand a certain or do not talk a certain way or hug someone a certain way. Hatred was never something I could ever feel for my parents and older brother for not understanding because it is what they were conditioned to think so i understood that yet for some reason I could not understand why people outside of my family get it probably because I was so focused on trying to fit in with everyone else when all I had to do was appreciate and love myself for who I am which I why I felt like I always needed to seek validation when it was not even necessary. My younger brother Andre was more of a go with the flow, so I do not think my sexuality bothered him as much as others in my family. For as long as I can remember without even realizing it, I put myself before me sacrificing some of my happiness and my peace so that they can have theirs in some way or some type of stability in their lives and in doing so I became taken advantage of because of it. It became like an addiction I couldn't shake like a programming. My friend eric and I always hung out at my house in my room playing video games and yes that was very fun but at some point, I wanted to do something else because after all friendships do not Soley only revolve around video games... After a while I started to settle and not care because I did not want to ruin the friendship by being negative, but it always came down to video games for him and that was the only reason he came over my house. As time went on, I convinced myself that he really was my friend and that maybe that was his way of validating our friendship. Certain people just clicked, well and we did. It is nice to have male and female friends that you can vibe with well. Those thoughts once again started to plague my mind again after my older brother Ronald and even my mom started to realize that was all it seemed like he was using me for but once again I had chosen to let it go until... I was hanging out with him and his girlfriend who had recently had a baby and his brother-in-law and for a while it seemed like we were all clicking, laughing, joking and just having a really good time. We were playing video games there and I suddenly started to feel really tired, so I took a nap and at one point I just opened my eyes, and I heard them talking as my supposed friends brother in law was looking me up on Facebook and once he found me I remember him saying very loud "IS THAT ISAAC!!!! HE IS SO UGLY!!!! Everyone started to laugh including my supposed friend. I felt so embarrassed that I did not want to get up off the floor so I pretended to still be asleep until they moved on to the next subject then I would make my move and get out of there and never speak to him again or hang out with those toxic people. I kept my word and I never hung out with them again. Over time the person I thought was my friend practically became a stranger to me. His dad was a very sarcastic man and i did not think he wanted him hanging out with me as much because of my sexuality so that could have played a small part in why our friendship dissolved. I started to become ever more so curious about my sexuality, wanting to experiment so I would go into gay chat rooms talking to guys online and I know how dangerous that can really be as there are tons of predators online. Some of the guys I met online I did experiment with but there was one I met on several occasions and one night we went back to his home, and it started out consensual but then I started to get a bad feeling and I wanted to stop and go home. There was no car for me to drive as I did not even have my license yet at the time. He told me to keep going and that he would take me home once I was finished and I told him no, I just wanted to go home now please but that was not enough to get through to him. Things started to get really tense as he started to yell at me" Your not done Yet!!!! I said keep going or I will you!!!! I'm not taking you anywhere! I started to cry as tears were running down my face and he started yelling at me again" I said shut up now or I will hurt you!! You're not.... going anywhere!!!! As his fist was so close to my face and I didn't know what to do because he could have had a gun, and he was already threatening so I did not have a choice but to give him what he wanted as the tears were running down my face as I was incredibly distraught over what happened. He told me to get in the car and I did, I would have walked but I did not know where I was at, it was so very dark. It could have taken me days to get home on foot, so I got in the car with him sitting on the edge of my seat wondering if he was going to hit me. Yes, I was wondering if this incredibly big strong guy was going to rip me apart. He didn't take me all the way home exactly but instead dropped me off on an incredibly dark road and said" Now get out of my car!!!! He practically pushed me out his car!!

CHAPTER 5

Friends? Or Bad influences?

*M*om was always a giver, helping those out in need of help and she even made some great friends along the way, there was practically nothing that mom and I did not do together but I started to get a strong feeling that one of her friends was not the right one that she should be hanging with. I discovered that she also had a drug problem which is something that my mom was battling against. One day my mom and her decided to go out shopping and the women that she was hanging out with decided to shoplift and to make matters worse my mom's so-called friend also had drugs in her car. The cops eventually pulled them over, my mom's friend was the driver, so she was the one who was facing more serious charges, but they did arrest my mom as well and she spent several weeks in lockup, and it devastated me. For those several weeks that she was away I was extremely sad and one day after school i was already dealing with bullies and they decided to all take a shot at me and they started calling me treacherous names and teasing me about my sexuality. As I ran home crying, I saw my mother who was finally home after being gone for weeks. I ran to her as she opened her arms and I opened mine so I could put them around her, I squeezed her so tight because the one person that I missed more than anything in the world was finally back. No matter what obstacle I was facing, just the mere presence of her made it go away so... my sad tears turned into happy tears as I knew God had returned her back to me. I know we are the gifts, the joys to our parents but my mom was my greatest joy, my greatest reward. Every second I was around her felt like a blessing. A mother always knows when there is something wrong with their kid so even though there were some happy tears, there was still some sad ones and knew so i told her what happened and she immediately wanted to go over to one of the bullies homes and talk to their parents about what happened and get him to leave me alone by talking to the parents. That's just how overprotecti ve my mom was not just for her kids but of everyone. She was a true warrior that was incredibly loyal and unstoppable. There was nothing that my radiant goddess of a mother could not conquer. She inspired me more than anyone else, always being that radiant light always helping others reignite that spark of light within everyone else. No matter how challenging things would ever get for her she never gave up, not in anyone else and most importantly she never gave up in herself and to me that is what it means to be a warrior, to keep on fighting for what you believe in, to keep on fighting to manifest the life that you want even in challenging times. No storm could stop her and I know that no storm will stop me from having the life that I want because I do have faith and I know that is where we are all the most powerful and no one could ever truly take her power away and no one will ever truly be able to take my power away either because I have the lord's grace within me and the grace is inspiring me to continue to inspire others to show them that there is a better path if they are open to it. I could never force someone to do something that they do not want but all I can do is continue to shine my light and that is something that I feel is brighter than ever. None of us can change the past no matter how hard we may want to, but we can live in the present and just go with the flow and not worry about the outcome of how things will be or should be but just embrace every moment. Every moment that we have on this planet is a gift but I also know that I cannot be anything to anyone else without being something to myself first and I'm learning to really embrace who I am and that is a kind, compassionate man that does the right thing and inspires others and even though I may make mistakes along the way and I will... I am just going to get back up every time like captain marvel, or doctor strange or iron man and even Thor. Those amazing superheroes inspire me to greatness along with my superhero mother. It was the year 2000 and i was starting middle school and I could not be more excited to be starting middle school. Every year that passed I was excited because it meant I was leveling up.

CHAPTER 6

Inspiring Teachers and New Friendships

I had some of the most amazing teachers and two were my favorite and they were miss miles and miss Biddle and the way they taught was so admirable. Miss Biddle would read books to us daily. She often read the harry potter books to us every day, so her class was always my favorite. She read everyone to us, and it was so interesting as I imagined myself in the harry potter universe. We were having a field trip to the Ren seance fair, and I was very excited because I love field trips and going on adventures. I was hanging out with two other classmates, and we wandered off from our chaperones and had a lot of fun exploring the fair. I could fill it in my gut that we were going to get into trouble. It was like I could feel the panic coming from my teacher because sure enough when we went back to the bus she was waiting for the bus when we came back, and she certainly whaled on us big time. She told us we were never allowed to go on another field trip again seeing as to how we wandered off. Her heart was beating so fast, I could feel it why my classmates were sitting on the bus looking smug. She certainly made it clear that she was going to tell our parents. The next day at school I did apologize for wandering off and I explained I was curious, and I loved to explore. She told me that she understood but that it was her responsibility to keep us safe and to please not try anything like that again. I wanted to give her a hug but for some odd reason that was prohibited in school. Even when I was in middle school that feeling that something big was coming that was going to change my life, something that would affect the world as well, but I often overlooked it once again. Miss miles my other teacher had the prettiest smile. I knew anyone that she encountered; her light would touch them. Another radiant teacher that inspired me to greatness. She never made any assignments too hard for us. We were always allowed to eat snacks in her class so that was awesome. I Started to make some good friends in middle school, and we always hang out at lunch. They were true genuine friends. One of my friends Zacary was having a sleepover and I got an invitation which was awesome. I was a bit nervous about the sleepover, but I did not let that stop me at all. When I arrived for the sleep over it went very well. Zach's mom was just so loving so we clicked right away. So that was my first time going on a sleepover and it certainly was not disappointing as it felt like an Adeventure, and I am a very adventurous person.

CHAPTER 7

Spending time with Dad

*E*very summer me and my brothers would go stay with my dad which I always enjoyed because he would spoil us like crazy when we were with him. My older brother liked to call him pops which I thought was kind of funny yet also interesting because it sounded very mature. Sometimes when I was around my dad I got a sense of feeling like maybe he wished things had turned out differently with mom but if there is one thing that I have learned is that you can't change the past but you can learn from it and grow into something amazing and keep on growing because when you think about it we all have a purpose and that is to live a liberating life free from the burdens of our past. They call it the past for a reason because it is behind you and they call it the present for a reason as that really is a gift that should always be cherished, and the future is something that we are all creating every single day. I also believe to have God's love, his amazing grace flow from within is a gift like no other and to me that is just wonderful magic. I always enjoyed it when dad gave me and Andre money to go to the store and once, we arrived back at his house we always had like 50 snacks much to my father's disappointment, but he just wanted us to be happy and content. My dad expected us to save up and use our money Wiseley which is what any parent who really loved their children would want. Ronald, my older brother OfCourse was still rebellious, and he was not always the only one as there were many times even as a kid, I would get me and my younger brother into some trouble unintentionally of course. Even when I got us in trouble my intentions were always good which is something my parents always knew about me because sometimes even when you do try to do good thing it can still backfire on you unfortunately and even when my older brother was out there getting into trouble as well let's just say I have never known a big brother that took care of us the way that he has nor have I known a father that would do anything just to make sure that his three sons were happy. Mom and dad always kept a good friendship even though they were not together. Me, Andre and Ronald enjoyed going to the movies with dad as he seemed to have good taste in movies that we also enjoyed watching at the movie theatre. Dad, like my older brother, was always overprotective with us as any parent should be so whenever I got into an argument with mom's boyfriend, and I called dad he would threaten to come up to where I lived and attack mom's boyfriend. Luckily that did not happen if after the dust settled dad and mom's boyfriend were able to make peace with one another. My father's girlfriend was very kind to me, and my brothers and we really enjoyed her company. She cooked amazing food for us and let us stay up late and watch Disney movies. Even though she treated us like we were a part of the family all I could think about Is I wish I was doing those things with my own mother, so I just counted the days down until we got to go home. When it was time for us to go home I desperately wanted to be home by 8pm because there was an episode of my favorite show that I wanted to see so bad and I had this portable tv that dad had bought for me for Christmas but the picture was not so clear so I was hoping we would be home by 8pm but that was not the case. My father kept asking what was wrong but I did not want to talk about it so my little brother just blurted it out that I was upset because we might not make it home in time so that I could watch the episode. The episode was about a woman trying to get back to her home dimension and she needed the chosen one's sisters' blood to do it. The chosen one's sister was a beautiful mystical energy who was sent to her to protect from this evil threat in the form of a sister. After the chosen one's, sister was captured, she could not take it anymore so she had a breakdown when she lost her sister and went into a catatonic state and her best friend who was a powerful witch was the only one that could get her out of it. She had to go into the chosen one's head and find her in her own subconscious and bring her back so she could rescue her sister and save the world again and she succeeded. That is why I wanted to get home so bad as I did not like to miss any episodes of my favorite show. Every time I watched the show I felt like I could relate to the character as someone that wanted to be normal just like everyone else but then discovering she has a higher calling and that she was never meant to be like everyone due to the fact that she was the chosen one and it was her destiny to save the world or like other shows that were about chosen ones that I felt drawn to. There are many shows and movies with characters that I just felt connected to. I also just feel connected to everyone all over the planet in ways I never thought possible. I did not make It home on time to see the episode that I had been waiting to see so me and my brother did kind of butt heads as I had to wait quite a few months just to be able to see the episode again. There were so many scenarios that were playing out in my head. Can I find the full episode online? Can I find the whole episode on YouTube? Or even find it in parts and try to play the parts in order and make sense of the episode. I did however find parts of the episode on YouTube. This is how desperate I became to see the episode, also because I love supernatural shows. All these wonderful characters from all these amazing shows and movies played such a inspirational role in my life that I will never forget. You feel so drawn to something and it makes you very curious about learning new parts about yourself. It is always okay to be curious about yourself because you never know what you might discover. There were many times in my life when I envisioned if I lived a life like them, like what it would be like if I was a chosen one myself. I have always been a very imaginative and creative person. People have always told me I was always special, and I could feel it. Some just thought of me as very weird but I soon realized yes, I am weird but that is also what makes me the wonderful man that I am today and that is something to never have to apologize for. I knew there were other people out there like me and that God would have sent down my path one day. If you know you are meant for more and that you have a greater purpose, then you must trust that and trust that God has wonderful things in store for you and to never forget that when one door closes another always opens. There is no storm that we cannot conquer as long as we have the strength to keep on going. It is never meant to be easy growing but that is what is so exciting and even sometimes scary about the future is not exactly knowing but having faith that good things will always find you as long as you trust your path.

CHAPTER 8

The failures and successes of high school

There were many things I excelled at in high school and like anyone else there were things I failed in in high school, but I never let that stop me. Math was never one of my favorite subjects as I found that very challenging. I do not see anyone as being stupid when it comes to learning something new and even if someone were to think that, well that is their problem. We are all uniquely made so whereas others may see the problem I say turn it into your cool new superpower. Because of my struggles with math, I was placed in a learning support class which was nice as I got to be around others who knew what it was like to struggle with a particular subject in school. As for the other subjects in school I became so good that I became part of the national honors society because I made honor roll every marking period. Mom was so proud of me each marking period I made the honor roll. I know that I am a very intelligent man and there nothing I cannot accomplish if I stay committed to what I am doing. Mom always treated me to dinner every time I made honor roll. Because I and other students did so well, we were given the opportunity to go skiing in the Poconos on a first-come basis and even though I was not the best at skiing it was just the thrill of doing it that made it so exciting. When we all made it to the Poconos I assumed skying would be a very easy but oh boy was I wrong as I failed at it multiple times but I did not let that stop me as I always get back up every single time I fall and that is something I apply to whatever I fail at. We are all here to live a liberating life free of any burdens. No one can tell us what we should do or who we are as we are the ones that get to make those choices. My classmates were laughing at me each time I fell but it was perfectly fine as I was laughing too so I looked at it like we were all just laughing together. Later after the trip when I finally got home, I told mom how exciting it was and how many times I fell, and she began to laugh and gave me a hug as I told her I wished she could have been there with me. The year was 2006 and I was nearing my graduation and we as seniors of course had to complete a graduation project and I remember my project was about animals specifically a German shepherd. I remember wanting to wright everything I could about German shepherds so I researched everything that I could, and it was soon time to present our projects to the class and although my teacher noted that I did a fantastic job I received a C on my project. I did not question why my grade was so low because I realized that it does not matter what other people think or say as what others think of you or even your work means nothing, and it is everything when it comes to what you think about yourself. I passed my graduation project so that was good enough for me. After our graduation projects were completed all we did every time we had class leading up to graduation was watch movies or not come to school at all as It did not really matter, it's not like we had any assignments. I was never really in school that much during my senior year as I got out at 10:45 to either go to work at McDonalds or simply go home on the days that I did not have to work. I had some extra credits which allowed me to go on work release as I was also going to a vocational school for animal science and technology. On days that I did not have to work, if I did not go home, I would go to the mall and just hang out by myself, I mean sometimes you must find a way to enjoy your own company. School was always out at 2:25pm so I would leave the mall just like I did before whenever I would skip school sometimes except, I was not ditching this time and I would take a regular bus from the mall back to my school and catch the school bus just so that I would have a ride back home. There were many people that signed my yearbook as some called me Hollywood in school and wrote it in my yearbook to some talking about good times, we had at Six flags great adventure. There were many people in school that I had much love and respect for, including my teachers. Mom had It engraved on my yearbook "congrats, love you mom" I loved looking at the front of my yearbook seeing what mom had written more than anything else in the yearbook. It was June 14, 2006, and it was time for me and my stepbrother to graduate. My mom's boyfriend's kids were staying with us at the time, so it was a total of about 7 people in the house. My ever so loving radiant godmother showed up for my graduation, my strong fearless father showed up for my graduation of course and many more of our family members. I was very nervous on graduation day especially when they called my name, but I certainly felt the love as everyone screamed and cheered me on and it meant so much to me knowing how happy my family was for me and I certainly was happy for myself. So as one journey ended with high school, it was time to begin a new one.

CHAPTER 9

Life After Highschool

After high school I just wanted to take a break for a while before going to college. As many times as I wanted to go to college after high school it pretty much turned into procrastination as I became a bit too comfortable. I just wanted to stay home and take mom as I wanted to make her a priority in everything as her happiness meant everything to me. Mom would continue to work, and I would do all the house cleaning because I knew when she came home, she would be so tired. Seeing that amazing smile on mom's face every day she came home from work meant everything to me in the world, I guess people would say I am very overprotective of her. My 17-year-old brother Andre just found out he was going to be a father and my older brother Ronald was living with his girlfriend and 2 sons. My stepbrother marquise was off to vocational school. Me, mom and another one of my stepsiblings would watch One life to Live and general hospital every day when we did not have to work, or mom and I would go to this very amazing restaurant called King Buffett. I couldn't help but shake the feeling that something was coming and that it would still have a profound impact not just on my life specifically but the entire universe. I could never think of mom's boyfriend as a bad guy I just could not shake that looming feeling that he would not be there when she needed him the most and I could never blame him for anything but that feeling was there. After yet another argument that he and mom had I just had about enough of him hurting her. He had always been a good Christian man and I know God used him to help my wonderous mom through some difficult times like when she would relapse and end up doing drugs again. It was so clear what a positive effect he was having on mom because she stopped doing drugs once and for all and she began turning to God. My older brother Ronald and his girlfriend decided to end their relationship and he eventually made the choice to resume his relationship with a old flame. After about a year she realized that she was pregnant, and my older brother was expecting his second child which I again predicted would be a girl just like his first child. Mom quit her job and decided that she wanted to stay at home full time. I was working at Mcdonalds still, but it was starting to not feel very fulfilling at all so I made the call to put in two weeks' notice as I would soon begin my new job at a video game store. That feeling was looming again that something was coming and not only was it going to affect my life, but it was going to affect the entire universe. I kept trying to make sense of what was happening. All I knew is It would be very bad. You ever have a strong feeling that you were going to change the world, someway? Somehow? It just felt like God was preparing me. Some dreams I had felt like they were warnings of dark things to come, a storm that was coming. There are many things that I wanted to talk about, but I did not how to explain them to anyone. Why do I feel connected to everyone and everything on the planet and animals? Where are these strong feelings I get when something does not feel right? Could the dreams I am having mean something more? The signs are always there, we just must be willing to listen. Why am I getting all these DeJa'Vu feelings? I knew that anyone I explained these feelings to would just tell me I am paranoid so I convinced myself that it was all in my head, but I could not truly let it go. I quit my job at the video game store and began working at Wendys where I was harassed and bullied by not only my manager, but I was also harassed and teased by another employee. The employee knew that I was gay so he would try making passes at me and then teasing me about. Once I told the manager about what was happening, she began teasing me about the situation as well. All anyone has ever told me was to stop being so sensitive or I am crazy like my feelings were not validated at all. After being teased in high school and being teased at McDonalds, Wendy's, even ones that I thought were my friends, I was beginning to feel so tired of always caring for others and wanting to take care of them without any real regard for myself. When I was in school, I was called retarded by people, when I was at work, I was either called ugly or a nobody queer. It came down to me realizing that if this is how people are in the world to survive then maybe I should be the same to survive. I started another new job after quitting Wendy's due to the harassment doing warehouse work and I made several new friends there. One friend Adam who I helped with rides to and from work seemed very cool until there were times he would get mad and take his frustrations out on me even going as far as to calling me a Black queer that should be dead. He wished death on me for being a black man and for being gay. His insults were becoming too much so I went to one of my bosses who told me that if I wanted to report him, I could go to the office and I told her no I did not want to do that but rather have someone talk to him and that it is it. I just wanted the whole thing to be over but unfortunately another one of my bosses was standing next to me and decided to go to the office and report him for what he said to me. If I ever even looked at Adam I would go to great lengths and tell me What the am I looking at when all I was simply doing was saying hi to him. Employees from the HR office came out into the warehouse to escort my friend off the floor for his harassment. I was beginning to feel very guilty and ashamed not only for how he made me feel for being who I am, but I was feeling guilty for getting him fired. Me and Adam stopped being friends of course after the incident but my guilt started to weigh heavily on me, so I called him and apologized many times, promising to help him get another job. I felt like it was my mission to try to fix what he caused in the first place. Adam said it's okay and he was not mad at me, but it became clear that he just wanted to continue to take advantage of me again. There were times he was in holding cells for his failure to pay his fines and I had to help him resolve it by helping him with rides to the grocery stores and to get his identification card from the driver's license center. After I realized that he was still manipulating me I had to release the toxic attachment for good. Even after I noticed he was stealing things from Walmart I still wanted to be there for him. After caring so much for others and becoming too tired of it I began to let the darkness in more and convinced myself maybe it is better to just live life like them, so I began making mistakes that were starting to take a toll on my life.

CHAPTER 10
The Stroke

After being hurt so many times, I was beginning to lose my way. Mom had another stroke and she had to go to physical therapy because of her leg. All I ever wanted to do was be there for mom so that she did not face any kind of stress and when she had health issues. She had just got into another argument with her boyfriend and just as I predicted he was not there for her during her time of need, so I made it my mission to make sure she had everything she needed for her recovery. One night after I came home from work there was a store that was opened past midnight and I remember mom asking me to go get her sweet Potatoe pie and I brought it back to her to eat and 30 minutes after she had her pie, I noticed something was off. Mom asked me again to go get her pie as I told her that I already bought it for her. She claimed that I never went to get it. It was my theory that the stroke may have affected her memory. To put her at ease, I went to go get her another pie only for the same thing to happen again. She claimed that I never went to get the pie. I helped mom up to use the bathroom and I ran downstairs to get some cloths out of the dry machine, as I was attempting to fold them, she was calling me to help her back up into the bed. I didn't hear her the first time, but I did the second time and I told her I was coming upstairs now and then she started to call me again and all of a sudden it got very quiet. I have always had these strong like I could sense when something is not right or sense when someone is hiding something or just not being honest. In my bones, I could feel it that something was not right with mom, so I dropped the clothes and ran upstairs only to watch in horror as mom was on the floor unconscious next to a heater that was off, but she could have hit her head. I screamed her name "Mom!!!!! Please wake up!!!!! Please!!!! I'm so sorry it's all my fault! As mom lay unconscious, I called 911 so distraught in tears and explained to them what happened. I managed to get her on her bed as I asked 911 what to do and they told me they were on their way. I had never been so frightened in my entire life. This incredible woman who was my moral compass and everything to me wasn't talking or moving. 911 had me check to make sure she was still breathing, and she was. The paramedics showed up and got her on the stretcher and took her to the hospital while I ran upstairs to change my clothes and rush off to go to the hospital. When I got to the hospital it took a few hours as they were still doing tests to find out what happened. The doctor soon came out to tell me that it was definitely another stroke. That guilt of what happened took a toll on me like nothing else ever has in my life. Once morning came around, they managed to get mom to her room and when I saw her, she had her eyes open but there were no words coming out of her mouth. I pleaded with her to please forgive me for what happened thinking that there had to have been a way to help her wondering what if I just made it up there sooner. Visiting hours were ending at the hospital so I had to go home to shower and change. After about a few weeks of mom being in the hospital she did manage to regain her voice but there were still some major complications from the stroke.

CHAPTER 11

Rehab

Mom was sent to a rehab facility to recover, and I was more determined than ever to fix what I felt was my fault. I was determined to save her life and I know at all costs. I knew somehow someway that I was going to save her life, I was going to make whatever sacrifice I had to for the sake of my mom. How could I not save the one person who has loved me unconditionally. Whenever I would ever be away from mom, I always still felt so connected to her, whether she was stressed or happy or any kind of emotion really. As I entered the rehab to visit mom why she was trying to recover, there was just this terrible feeling I was beginning to get, it was clear that there was something wrong with mom and I heard a woman screaming way down the hall before I got there. She was screaming in agenizing pain and when I entered her room, I told her I would be right back, and I ran to get the nurse only for them to tell me that she was not due for her medicine yet. I had to watch this beautiful woman with so much heart and soul scream and look so weak and tired. It was like part of my mother was there and the rest was just gone. I know what her pain was like because I felt it, and I begged God with everything in my soul to heal her and leave me in that bed. I know it isn't what she would have wanted but I just wanted her to be able to live her life again. Mothers make sacrifices for their children, so I was going to do it for her. No matter what anyone told me I was not going to accept defeat. All that I wanted to do was take her home and never leave her again but also that she needed to be in the rehab to get better. In my heart and soul, I knew that if the doctors could not do anything then God would find a way. I also know that even after you have tried everything that you could that all that you can do now is leave the rest up to the lord. As a child I made a vow that anyone who could not be there for mom and take care of her especially when she is sick or stress that I would be there. Mom's smile, mom's laugh made me incredibly happy, but that smile was no longer there, that laugh was no longer there, and I was determined to make sure she got it back. I am not someone that believes in the impossible as I believe all things are possible, you just have to believe so I believed that even if I had to go all the way around the world that I would find a way. How could I not save the best friend that I ever could have asked for who has saved me more times than I could count. My younger brother was in school, and he eventually saw mom in her condition, and I wanted to give him hope that I would save her. My older brother was away in lockup, and I know how much he was hurting because he could not get out to see her so I gave him hope that I was going to find a way to restore her to the person that she use to be or at least partially to where she could be happy.

CHAPTER 12

Coming home

The time had come for mom to come home, I could feel how happy she was to be returning home. We were both happy that she was coming home, and I knew what a challenge it would be, but I did not care so long as she was home with her family where she belonged. It was just me and mom most of the time as my youngest brother was still away in school and my oldest brother was away as well. Mom and her boyfriend were still broken up at the time and his kids went with him when he moved out. I wanted mom to feel as loved and safe as possible and it was clear she would feel that when she was at home. Mom continued to have constant pain and was treated with pain medication. My daily tasks for taking care of mom were to feed her, bath her, give her medications as needed and just enjoy some quality time with her doing what we always loved to do which was watch lifetime movies or horror/sci-fi movies. We loved a movie with a good mystery. Even before mom got sick, I always predicted what the outcome of the movie would be or what would happen with specific outcomes when we watched our soap operas. We had a couple of caregivers there for mom for just a few short hours during the day and a few during the night which were a few of mom's close friends while I worked my full-time job. I was becoming mom's power of attorney, so I made sure her finances were taken care of and helped with her doctor's appointments. It wasn't easy juggling so much and still working full time not to mention I was doing as much research as possible on other victims of strokes like mom's condition that suffered from strokes that made recoveries. I knew that if they had the same condition and recovered then there was hope that mom would recover. There was additional research. I did about possible treatments that could help her. There were doctors that I spoke to as well to get a 2nd or 3rd opinion after I got the devastating news from mom's primary doctor that she would never walk again on the phone that she would never walk again. When the doctor told me the news it felt like my world had shattered into a million pieces as I went into work attempting to hold it together at least until the end of my shift but within five minutes I was already falling apart. Mom was in the hospi tal again because of some complications. I burst into tears, and I remember the room just spinning as I passed out. There were two coworkers that managed to get me to the HR office and when I came to the HR managers were questioning me about what happened, and I explained to them that mom was sick due to several strokes. The HR manager upset me in a significant way because she implied that if I could not get it together that I cannot come back to work. I could always pick up on things like when someone is saying one thing, but they are thinking another thing. It is safe to say that I was a human lie detector. It felt like the manager was stating that I needed to get over what was happening with my mother because their business was much more important. I realized that I could no longer working there was going to work for me seeing as to how these human beings are more focused on their business then having some compassion, so I walked out because I was not going to work there under those circumstances, and I know mom needed me more. I was still not feeling well after the incident and a friend drove me to the hospital to get checked out and be with my mother. Once I arrived at the hospital I got checked out and then I went to go be with mom in her room until the time came for them to release her so she could come back home. My godmother and brothers wanted to know how she was doing so I explained to them what happened and I assured them that no matter what even if I had to go to the ends of the earth I would find a way to save mom, I mean how could I not, this angelic woman has saved me more times than I could ever count and has loved me unconditionally. I know that is how a mother is supposed to care for children, but my mom truly is the best friend that I could have asked for. I knew that if I held on and had faith that she would one day be okay, and I wanted to give my family hope that she would be okay one day because I could feel their pain as well no matter how far away in the world. Some friends and family suspected that I might be psychic seeing as to how I could pick up on so much or feel so connected to so many people. My priority was still to focus on mom at the time and help her recover by any means necessary. Even when all the doctors told me there was nothing I could do, I would have found a way no matter what because that is how much I love her. It did not matter what the doctor's thought was impossible because I told myself that anything is possible, and I could be a very stubborn person so hearing the world "no it is not going to happen "meant nothing to me as there is always a way and I knew that one day I would find it

CHAPTER 13

Saving Mom

I knew that I was going to save mom's life at all costs. My first task was looking into other's cases who have had similar conditions like mom, As I continued my research, I discovered that there were other individuals who suffered from massive strokes and either made a full recovery or a partial recovery. Mom was beginning to give up and I needed to give her some hope that she was going to make it. I prayed every night that the lord would heal my mom from her sickness. The devil wanted us to give up by I was not about to allow it to have power over either of our lives. Even when mom's primary doctor told me there was no hope and that mom would never recover, I just felt the lord's presence within me willing me to keep on going and to keep on believing. I know that whatever happens is up to God, but I just wanted my mother to have her life back more than anything in the world. My determination to save mom's life made me realize that she was going to need me more than ever, so I was willing to sacrifice my relationships of any kind whether that was a friendship or a romantic relationship. After a while I realized that mom would not have wanted that so while we had caregivers that I hired for mom for just a few hours I attempted to have a romantic relationship as I was still trying to find a way for mom to recover. I began a relationship with someone, but it became too difficult to maintain that relationship and when it came time for that relationship to end, I took it badly. I had lost so much in my life due to losses in my family, losing my confidence to bullies, mom slipping away and so much more. After being treated horribly by so many you start to question things. There have been great successes in my life, but I was beginning to feel like the bad was outweighing the good. Many people have told me that I was incredibly ambition and I was going to use that ambition to save mom. My romantic relationship ended and after some time had passed, I realized it was for the best as I could put my attention one hundred percent towards her. No one wants to hear their mom scream and shout why this had to happen to her. My mom has always been a warrior so now it was my turn to be a warrior for her. She was in the hospital at least twice a week due to complications that she was having and every time I went to visit, I could feel her agonizing pain from down the hallway. I continued to ask God if he could please have me be the one that was in the bed and not mom but still nothing happened. I wanted God to punish me because I did not make it upstairs in time to help mom before she fell on the floor. I begged him as the tears came running down my face. Once mom was back home from the hospital once again, I decided to try another approach. I convinced myself that maybe I could make a video and post it online and that maybe a doctor would see it and find a way to save her or someone who has suffered the same condition that could help us. No one reached out so I just continued to investigate other's conditions like moms, but I did not have any luck. I did some research about Jefferson hospital in Philadelphia, and I gave them a call as they specialized in helping people with severe strokes. When I called and had mom's condition explained to the doctor, he said there may be something that can be done but he would not know for certain until he saw her. That was enough to give me more hope and that was enough to give mom more hope as well. It felt like we were finally getting somewhere. After about a few weeks the time had come to take mom to Jefferson hospital. She was so weak and tired, so I knew that it was crucial to get her there. My younger brother was home on a break from school, so he was able to drive us there why I carried mom and got her into the car. Once we got to the hospital and I walked her into the office, I remember how everyone was looking at us waiting to see their doctors as mom sat in her wheelchair looking so frail and weak as the Patin continued to get worse severely in her legs. I could feel everyone's sorrow as they watched as I pushed her into the waiting room. I felt like I was going to die. Mom could barely sit up in her wheelchair. No matter what, I had to stick to my mission and save mom's life. The doctor finally called us in so that he could look at mom and I was already beginning to get a bad feeling that it was not going to turn out well. I could feel the emotions that were coming from the doctor. He examined mom and it took all but five minutes for him to say that there was nothing that he could do. As the doctor gave us the terrible news, I burst into tears begging him to please save her and that I would pay anything whatever it took if he could help her. The doctor again told me there was nothing he could do. Once I got mom back in her wheelchair and wheeled her through the lobby with everyone watching us, I just couldn't give my brother the terrible news so I told him that it did not go so well but it was not all bad and that we just must keep on taking care of mom. I told my older brother the same thing as he was still in prison. No matter what, I was never going to give up trying to save the light of my life no matter what the circumstances were. Where there is will there is always a way, and I was going to continue to find that way as I promised her. I discovered that there was a way to help her through other people's strokes and aside

CHAPTER 14

Loss

*M*om's condition began to get worse, and I felt like time was beginning to run out. She would not eat her breakfast, lunch or dinner and then it suddenly happened again. She had another stroke!!! This time she lost the ability to speak at all without any chance of ever regaining her voice. I immediately called 911 and they came to take my mom to the hospital as I remained at home and got dressed so that I could go see how she was doing. When I arrived at the hospital and right before I even looked at mom's face, I could feel her pain and then I looked at her and she could not say a word. She was trapped without the ability to walk and the ability to speak and all I wanted was for her to come home. When the time came for mom to be released from the hospital, everything was different. Mom now had to be fed through her tube and the aide that we did have there for just a few short hours was not authorized to feed mom through the tube and I did not know how to do it. I knew mom did not want to be fed through the tube and I did not know what else to do until she ended up in the hospital yet again. Every doctor that I spoke with told me that I did everything that I could and that the only thing left to do now was to send mom to a nursing home. I was beginning to realize that maybe they were right and that there was nothing more that I could do, and I went into mom's hospital room, and I begged her to please forgive me as the tears came running down my face. I said "mom please I am so sorry, please don't hate me but

I did everything that I could, please mom just tell me what to do. I tried finding treatments through other's cases that may be able to help mom, I looked online every day for ways for mom to recover, I tried calling doctors in Philadelphia that specialized in people with multiple strokes, I took her to specialists, and I even tried posting a video on YouTube hoping that someone would reach out and be able to help me with mom's condition. Once she had another stroke it was just beyond my control, so I had to send her to a nursing home, and I felt like I failed her, and I did not know how I was going to move past that. I felt like I had failed my mother when I promised her that I would take care of her. She was sent to a nursing home, and I began making terrible choices to cope with the pain. Once mom was sent to a nursing home and I went to visit her it just felt like she wasn't there anymore. She could open her eyes but that was all. Her life was never going to be the same again as she would be fed through a tube. I was beginning to lose my faith. I became angry and I did not want to be around anyone. A few weeks later I woke up in the morning and something felt off, it was as if my mom had moved on, I could just feel it, my mom was gone, and I knew it. I looked at my phone and I have over 20 missed calls and I called the nursing home where mom was staying and then confirmed my worst fears that in January 2014 my mother had passed away. I informed as much of my family as I could who were also great friends of my mom's, but I just couldn't let go of the guilt. It took me some time but eventually I was able to let go of the guilt of what happened to mom and many others have told me that it was not my fault when mom had her first stroke and fell on the floor when I ran downstairs to get something out of the machine. I found peace and more importantly she has found peace because God has called her home to be with him in the light. God knows that I did everything that I could for her, and I know that he is now taking care of her and that makes me so happy, and I know that one day we will see each other again but until then, living a happy fulfilling life is what she would have wanted. My mother was the light of me and my brother's life as well as family and friends and I will honor her. Mom may have left the land of the living, but I truly could feel her spirit around me. Getting through the funeral was one of the most difficult things because the guilt of what happened to her started to take a toll on me some more and I could feel everyone else's emotions heavily. Once the funeral was over, we went to go eat and I for one do not understand how anyone could eat something right after a funeral, I for one could not eat. My younger brother was headed back off to school, my older brother wanted to make sure that we were taken care of. I was beginning to lose myself and I begin to let the darkness take hold of my life, so I started to make some very bad choices because I wanted to feel anything other than pain and no matter how many times, I felt like I was escaping it I was right back where I started. I started to go into the darkness more and more and I began making terrible choices with drugs and shoplifting. I was beginning to feel like so much was taken from me, and my family and I became determined to never let it happen again, so I put up more walls because I felt like it was the only way to keep myself and them safe.

CHAPTER 15
The darkness

*A*fter mom died, I put up many walls, making a vow that I would never let anyone take anything from me or my family ever again. I began hanging out with friends who I initially did not think were necessarily into drugs but when I realized it, I became tempted. It's not something I ever thought about doing but once mom died I felt a big hole in my heart and I just wanted to make the pain go away for a little while or as long as I could and once you get a taste of the hard drugs it can sometimes be hard to let go and that is exactly what happened in my case. I could never blame anyone because at the end of the day it was always my choice to make. At first me and this man who I thought was my friend were just smoking marijuana and then he mentioned hitting the streets to look for heroine so I drove us to a city in Philadelphia where we would be outside looking for hours for someone to sell to us. There were times we get the drugs and come back to the car and start doing them and pass out and wake up in the morning not really remembering what happening. I would drive him home in the morning and later in the day we would meet back up and hit the streets again at night looking for drugs. When we started doing the drugs again the man I I was hanging out with whose name was Joshua completely freaked out after he did his dose of heroin and started running around the city and then ran back to my car claiming that someone was chasing him, and he quickly got into my vehicle, and we drove off. We would go looking for these drugs practically every day. One night after he freaked out and fainted in the middle of the street and I immediately called 911 as they took him to the hospital. I didn't know him that well as I was just looking to hang out with someone and get high smoking marijuana which was illegal at the time. We both wanted something stronger, he just had more experience with drugs then I had thought. Once 911 picked Joshua up and took him to the hospital I forgot to ask which hospital he was in so I basically called every hospital that I could think of to make sure that he was okay. I knew that he was worried that his parents would find out and I could not leave him there alone. I had convinced myself that I was going to take him home and that we would never hang out again, but I try to see the good in everyone, so I gave him another chance which only led to us getting high again. He contacted me because he wanted to meet up and hit the streets looking again and I accepted, only this time I was the one on the other end. We started hanging out in a motel this time and we started getting high yet again and then I blacked out. When I came to in the morning he was gone! This same man who I made sure got to the hospital after he overdosed and made sure was okay and safely got back home had left me alone in a motel to die. When the paramedics finally got me to wake up, I do not think there ever another more frightening thing that ever could have happened to me in my life other than what mom had to go through. The paramedics began to ask me as I slowly opened my eyes "Do you know where you are? You almost died but we were able to bring you back." I kept asking "where is Joshua, "what happened"? as they told me that the person who cleans the rooms found me like that. I could not understand how someone could be so cruel as to let me die. The paramedics took me to an ambulance, and I remember just feeling so weak and barely able to talk. As the ambulance was taking me to the hospital, I began to black out again only to wake up in a hospital room again being questioned by a strange man asking me what happened with a clip board and a paper. The man told me i was not allowed back in the

area where the incident happened, but I had to go back to get my car. Once the man got done questioning me, I began to black out again and came to later at night. When it came time for me to be discharged, I did not have any transportation to get back to the motel where my car was parked so the hospital provided me with a voucher to get back. Once I arrived back at the motel, I saw that my car was gone so I went to the front desk of the motel, and I was informed that my car had been towed and there was nothing that could be done about it until morning. The motel had my wallet which they returned, and I had no way of getting home so I had to get to a motel outside of the city for the night and retrieve my car in the morning and then go home. Once I woke up in the morning it was time to go get my car and once I arrived at the place where my car was towed I had to pay about a thousand bucks to get it back, I didn't care as I just simply wanted to get home but that was not the only thing on my mind as all I kept thinking about getting high with heroin again, the same drug that nearly took my life I was craving to try again and again. I became so addicted, and I did not know how to stop, and I was going to do everything that I could to get high again somehow and someway because it made me feel less pain.

CHAPTER 16

The darkness
Part 2

After Losing mom I continued to make poor decisions and hanging out with the wrong people as I further let myself get further influenced. I started hanging out with someone in Philadelphia who genuinely seemed kind at first until it was revealed that he was into snorting coke. At first it seemed like we could have one day been the best of friends as we talked about our pasts and how we had been hurt and picked on by other people. There were several disagreements that we did end up having which led to arguments due to a lot of miscommunications. We snorted coke quite a few times together. After a while we lost touch and somehow reconnected in 2022 but his personality had seemed very different from when we first met. It turned out he was doing crystal meth which I also ended up doing with him several times, but I still feel as though he had ill feelings towards me because of past arguments. It was as if he never let it go yet somehow was manipulating me. It is something that I just felt but could never really explain. One day I came back over, and we got high yet again with what I thought was crystal meth again as I loved doing it but this time when we started doing it something had felt incredibly different. It felt 10 times worse than what we had tried before. I began to lose my balance like I was going to pass out, the room began to spin, and I could barely get a sentence out of my mouth as he looked incredibly smug asking him what he did, what did he put in the pipe. There was this smirk on his face as though he enjoyed seeing me falling apart. I screamed and yelled at him, claiming that I would call the police and report him, but I had no concrete proof. It was clear that this man had drugged me so that I could fall apart and look crazy, knowing that if I said anything I may look like I was weird. Once I got out of there, I drove him under the influence as everything was still praying that I would get back without getting into a car accident. When I arrived home called him back several times trying to get some type of proof to go to the police and let them know what happened. I was so distraught from whatever drug he gave me that I could not return to work for a few days as I did not want to lose my job as it was my only source of income. I know I made my own choice to get high in the first place, but I never thought he would take advantage of me in that way. As I was driving around at night I stopped at a park, and I was roaming around saying things hysterically as I saw a man parked by the sidewalk on his motorcycle. Something felt off like maybe he was watching me, and I knew it was not the drugs because I had been seeing people show up certain places that I would be traveling to. It just felt like someone was watching me. There were people I would begin to encounter that seemed genuinely kind almost as if they were trying to protect me. It felt like the universe was trying to keep me safe and help me get back on my destined path. There were also times I met people that I felt like were out to make sure I do not want to see me get to where I was beginning to feel like God was trying to lead me. Things were getting much worse for me as I was hanging out with another group of people and I decided to get high once more to mask what I was really feeling and once I did, I let myself enjoy it too much and the person I was hanging with let me sleep there as I could not drive but I left at night anyway and I started to notice I was being followed yet again by not just one specific person but several people. Once again it felt like they were trying to keep me safe. I stopped my car and began walking in the middle of the night without my shoes on. As I was walking, I was high but lucid enough to know what I was doing, I just didn't care because i was losing my faith in everything. An ambulance drove by and stopped and checked me out as I told them I was fine, and I wanted to go home, and they let me go until a police officer drove by and picked me up. They were going to take me back to my car but then they started questioning me and I told them a lie about what I was doing and with what drug hoping I would not and up in jail, but the lie did not help any as they arrested me anyway and took me to a holding cell. Tight small spaces is something that always bothers me, and I felt like I could not breath and someone answered on the intercom saying everything was going to be okay and that someone would be by in the morning and let me out and they did the next morning. Some lie for their own selfish means, but I felt like I had to tell certain lies to survive and protect myself from ever getting hurt again. Peace has always been something that I have wanted but it just became so much harder to hold on to after everything that I have had to put up with and all the losses. Once I left the police station, I walked back to my car which took me a while to find. Not only was I given a massive fine to pay off, but I had a court date that I now had to deal with. I told myself that I was going to put it all behind me, but the addiction was beginning to take over yet again as I was craving more drugs.

CHAPTER 17

The aftermath, am I clairvoyant?

*A*s I drove home after the whole ordeal, I began starting to feel like someone was following me yet again. Every time I looked around, I couldn't exactly tell but it was just a feeling I would get. I tried turning up different roads to see if they would follow me, but they did not. When I arrived home and parked out back and went inside, I was calling my roommate's name to see if he was home, but no one was there or so at least I thought. I knew he was there because it felt like someone was in the house. There were several vehicles parked out back and they were watching my home. I panicked and freaked out and ran out of the house and right to the hospital as I was having a packed attack. What I have realize now is that there were people looking after me because they thought I may be a danger to myself and possibly others. Once I arrived at the hospital, I started to get another bizarre feeling. No one was around in the hospital to be found as I went to several floors screaming that someone was after me and I needed their help as well as the police's help. I did not think to call the police at the time because I was in such a panic. Once I finally found a nurse and explained what happened, she looked at me like I was on drugs and crazy and to be honest she was not entirely wrong. The nurse took me down to the emergency room and they checked me out and wanted to draw blood. I knew they were going to find out that I was doing drugs, and I was going to be in a lot of trouble. As I continued to freak out after they drew my blood, something just felt off even more about the way the doctors were talking. I heard someone talking in the next room about a weird guy outside in the middle of the night saying all kinds of crazy things and that they should have me sent to a hospital for a 72-hour evaluation. The only thoughts that were crossing my mind is I dare them judge me, they had no idea what I had been through, and I wanted to go home. The doctors were waiting for the results to come back after they took my blood, and I told them do not to worry, I wanted to leave now. It felt like they kept stalling, waiting for someone to come back and do an evaluation on me. Getting put in a mental hospital was something that terrified me so I told them that if they did not let me go home now, I would leave regardless. I did not care about paperwork or anything. They stated that if I left, I would not be allowed to go back there. Once I arrived back at home, my roommate was there in his bedroom, but I began to get another strange feeling like maybe he was hiding out because he was informed that I was doing drugs and acting erratic. When I went to my bedroom, I got into the bed, I still felt like someone was watching me and I looked out the window and it was an old friend hiding behind a bush watching through my window. It was becoming clear that if they could not watch me in a hospital then they would watch me outside my home. I looked out my window several times as he stood behind the bush peaking though my window to try to see what I was doing. I called Adele who has always felt like a second mother to me, and we could talk just about anything. She is so loving and so compassionate and is truly a remarkable gift to this world. I told her about what happened at the hospital, and she wanted to ask me a question that I was not ready to answer. She wanted to know if I was on drugs, so I told her the truth that I was, but I was detecting something else like maybe she knew more than she was willing to tell. I told her that I was considering going to rehab and that I would call around looking for one to get into. There was one in Florida, and I wanted to know If I could stay with her for a while which she gladly accepted because she lived in Florida. The rehab center in Florida told me that they had a room for me in Florida. Eventually I declined and changed my mind as I was told I could check out outpatient services where I could get help in a different way. When I drove to the outpatient services center, I knew I was still being followed, I could just feel it. When I went into the center to get an evaluation and came out, I knew I was still being followed and watched only not as much. When I arrived home one of my neighbor's kids walked up to me asking for ice cream which I would always give because I always had a way with the kids, probably because I am a kid at heart. His mom walked up to him and told him to come inside but I was feeling something yet again like his mom did not want him around the addict and that started to break my heart because I have always had so much love for the kids and their family. A lot of people make mistakes, bad choices, but in my opinion if you do not know their story then do not be so quick to think the worse of them. Everyone in the town began to treat me like some freak addict who was volatile. The only thing that I could do was move past it and try to heal the best way that I can. I began getting outpatient services like counseling and I got a psychiatrist that would prescribe me medications. During my counseling sessions I shared part of what led me there and heard other's stories about what led them there as we were all on a journey of healing.

CHAPTER 18

Ronald returns and old habits dies hard

*A*fter going to outpatient services and having counseling sessions and hearing others talk about their stories felt really inspiring. I knew that it would be hard but that somehow, I would be okay. There was a huge part of me that still struggled with letting go of the past and how people treated me and as time went on the pain began taking over again and I wanted to get high again. I began hanging out with another group of people who were doing hardcore drugs, and the temptation began taking over again so I gave in and began getting high again to deal with past pain. As I continued to lose control and give into the drugs again, I let it once more nearly drive me over the edge again. When I left the group of people that I was hanging out with I was so high I could barely see, and I still had to drive home. I drove as slow as I could, but I had to pull over several times as I began to feel incredibly sick to my stomach. I shouted for someone to help me or call 911 but no one came so I shut the door and began driving slowly again just praying that God got me home safely. There was no way I could keep on driving, so I made the decision to once again pull over and call a friend to come get me. Once my friend Renee showed up, he managed to get me home and eventually we got my car back home. I was so ashamed of myself for relapsing, and I began to feel like all hope was lost once more. There was no way I could bring myself to work for a few days as it took me some time to come down from the drugs. No matter what happened, one thing I could never do is come to work under the influence as I always wanted to keep my work life separate from my personal life. Sharing that I relapsed was not a option for me at counseling sessions or with the psychiatrists. I began hitting the streets looking for others that I could buy some drugs with to get high anytime I could and there were times I either succeeded or failed to get some. I started to becom e more distant and didn't even want to hang out with little friends I did have either because I was high or coming down from the drugs. Things were getting so bad that I began shooting up drugs to mask the continued pain. I stopped going to see my psychiatrist every week and by then I had already completed my counseling sessions. Working started to become more difficult for me to go to so I notified human resources that I needed to take a leave of absence due to some personal issues. My older brother Ronalds wrote every chance he could get, and he was soon coming home so I wanted to prepare everything for when he did arrive home. I wanted to move where I lived as I felt like attempting to start over, but I paused things until my brother came home from jail and got settled in. Close friends and family helped with setting up a welcome home party for him, while my younger brother Andre had returned home from college announcing that he and his girlfriend were getting married and that she was also pregnant. My younger brother was expecting his second child, and I could not have been more thrilled for him. Friends and family did all the planning with getting the food ready for Ronald. My only responsibility was to make sure the home looked nice and today for him. Dad was also on his way to Ronald's welcome home party. Everyone gathered at the house and soon enough Ronald showed up and walked through the door we were so thrilled to have him with us. Thoughts of what it could have been like for my older brother in prison while mom was sick. I began to feel the guilt plague me again of failing mom and failing everyone else as I promised them that somehow and someway, I would save mom's life. As Ronald began getting settled in his room, I began looking for ways to go out and get high. Ronald needed help with getting a job and he was unable to work with me at my job due to the fact he had a felony on his record so I began doing some research and making some calls to see if there was a job out there that would accept him with a felony. Eventually he found a decent job at a restaurant as a cook, and I was very happy for him. There were a few times he would have a co-worker bring him home from work and there were times I picked him up and dropped him off at work. The time had come for me to return to work after my leave of absence came to an end. They say brothers and sisters fight at times and that was the case with me, and my older brother got into several arguments and even fought when he was home. Ronalds eventually rekindled a relationship with an old girlfriend with whom he had a daughter with. This was Ronalds second daughter. He eventually moved out with his girlfriend, and they soon began facing issues in their relationship. The two ended their relationship and my brother moved back into the family home. There were times we continued to butt heads and fight and argue, and we always bounced back. Ronald once again was seeing his old girlfriend that he lived with until they decided that it was time for them to simply end things for good.

CHAPTER 19

Shoplifting

After a while, I would have just done anything to cope with the continued pain that I was feeling. When you become tired by being hurt by others and losing the people that you love at one point you start to lose yourself. You can call it conditioning or whatever you want but I started shoplifting because it gave me some kind of rush. Shoplifting was something that I promised myself I would never do but after seeing other supposed friends do it, I felt tempted so decided to go for it myself. There were times I got in trouble for shoplifting promising myself that I would never do it again until the hurt started to take over. I could hear God's voice trying to convince me otherwise. There were several occasions where the police would take me away in handcuffs. I know I cannot turn back the clock and I wouldn't want to but what I can do is take the mistakes that I have made as lessons. You go into a store, and you see something that you want and then I would start to think, "why shouldn't I take this? After all, so much was already taken from me, so I am taking something back". I know that is no excuse but those were the thoughts that were lingering in my mind. It became something that I just kept on doing pretty much on a weekly basis. There were times I was broke and didn't have a job and it would come down to food or sometimes an electronic device that I went and stole and practically every time I got into some kind of trouble. A lot of people may think or say otherwise but I knew I had sacrificed so much so I was going to take it back because I was tired of feeling the way that I was. There were times I got into trouble for shoplifting and seeing the police take me out and I saw everyone walking by me looking at me like I was some kind of criminal, and I was because after all I did commit a criminal offense. The police took me in and placed me in a holding cell where I either stayed for a few hours or for the night. After the police came and released me, I promised myself that I would never do anything like that again but then the temptation and the pain would always come back, and I would repeat the same mistake, risking getting me into a lot of trouble yet again. My mother always taught me how wrong shoplifting was. Sometimes I would have to appear in court for shoplifting and would have community service and there were times where I would let go with just a fine to pay. There were managers in certain stores where they told me that I was never allowed to come back, and I could not blame them for coming to that decision as I would have said the same thing if anyone stole from my store. Some of the stores where I shoplifted, I even call back confessing that I did shoplift, some of which were probably aware, and I asked them if I could work for them, it wasn't like I had a job at the time. If I did have a job, I would have asked them if we could set up a payment plan, but they just told me to not come back at all. All that could be done was for me to move on and try my best to never do it again, but I carried the pain with me causing me to make the same mistakes. I do not believe that anyone is the devil, but it can corrupt your soul like a sickness. My pastor has talked about in church why we need to have great faith, it's not about objects or anything but rather about trusting that God's light, his love will always lead you to victory. He is always putting pieces into place for our good. I know Jesus loves me unconditionally and I love him unconditionally as things have always worked in my life one way or another thanks to him which is why we must patient and always trust his timing. There is no storm that we cannot weather and there is nothing that we cannot conquer as the creator of the universe always has our best interest in mind. Even when things get difficult, we must remember that it is all part of the journey and we are being tested but this is where you must have great faith that a higher power is taking care of you, we must be willing to listen. No path is meant to be easy, that is the point, but things do get better over time. In my opinion, if you truly do feel like you are meant for more, then that is God calling you into your purpose.

CHAPTER 20
Marriage

It was 2017 and I kept telling myself that I was going to get my life together, so I gave it another shot. A lot of people say you should be careful who you are talking to online because there are a lot of predators on there. I gave myself a chance to try online dating and I met someone who seemed very charming. The relationship progressed quicker than I expected and one night when I came home, he called me crying his eyes out claiming that he had to go back home. It was unclear what exactly he meant until he told me that he was in the U.S. on a visa and that the only way for him to stay would be if we got married. Something just did not feel right, like maybe I was being manipulated or something, but I ignored my intuition and said yes that we could get married. It did not feel right but I went for it anyway because I did not want to deny someone the chance to live out their dream and have the life that they had been longing for. I convinced myself that maybe down the road I would feel like I did the right thing by agreeing to get married. I never liked to disappoint people and I felt like if said no I would be killing this man's dream so I said yes, I would do it, especially considering he poured his heart out to me over the phone. There were several friends that told me I needed to really think about it, and I knew before they ever even said anything that it did not quite feel right to me. You know in your heart and soul when someone is right for you, and I just didn't feel it in my heart but once again I convinced myself that I would get there. There is a difference between having love for someone and truly loving someone with all your heart and soul and I just didn't feel that way so I told myself it would take time and I would get there. Packing my life up and moving to a new town and moving in with someone and getting married was just a lot for me and it was too soon. There were things that just did not feel right around this man as he wanted me to not hang around certain friends of me and only be around his family and friends or arguments we would have and then I would bring up later and he would say to me "what are you talking about" I never said that. There was an occasion when I was in the room and said something to me and I just got a bad feeling and said to him that I did not like the energy in the room and he just gave me this ominous look, so I left the room and immediately felt better. I cannot deny the fact that I can be toxic sometimes as I have made many mistakes in the marriage, and I take full accountability for my actions. A lot of people would tell me that I could be very overly sensitive, and they were right. We were making frequent trips to the immigration office so that he could obtain citizenship status and he kept a lawyer on retainer for what I thought was until he obtained citizenship, but I began to get a strange feeling about that as well. There were times he ghosted me after some arguments that started because I was being overly sensitive but there was this feeling like maybe he was enjoying the fact that I was suffering. There were times it felt like he was trying to show the world that I was crazy. The wedding day had arrived and yet again it was beginning to not feel right in my gut about getting married. My intuition was telling me that a part of him knew that as I could really feel it, but he did not care because he had his eyes on the prize. The wedding began and the only thoughts that were roaming in my mind were "what am I doing? This is wrong? I can't breathe. I then told myself to just get it over with and no one should be thinking that way on their big day. Several years after the wedding and many arguments and yes even some cause by my mistakes I realized that I could not do it anymore as I was never happy, and I had to be fair to both of us. When I came home from work one night after midnight I began to drive home, and I realized I needed to tell him that I did not want to be married any longer. As I sat down to tell him, he again began to break down in tears, so I took it back and said I didn't know what I was thinking and to forget what I had said but then He said something else that was very strange.

He then said to me "so I can stay here and continue my studies"? I begin to think what do your studies have to do with us wanting to end the marriage? It just did not make any sense to me. Once again, I had chosen to ignore it as I was incredibly tired and wanted to sleep. My mistakes were my mistakes and I hate that I had to bring them into the marriage, but I have let that all go as I am finally on the right path,, and I know God is bring the right people in my life an removing the wrong ones from my life as everything has a purpose. I now realize that it was all part of the journey to go through the bad to get to the good. The marriage went on and I continued to live in denial that maybe I could make it work but it honestly seemed like he was playing some kind of psychological mind game with me as I could not tell the difference between right or wrong anymore or if I really was crazy as I began to question everything and lose my grip on reality.

CHAPTER 21

Something just does not feel right

There were times I could be incredibly stubborn and did not want to go out. It was not because I did not like anyone but more about the fact that I simply get overwhelmed being around a lot of people. It was September 10, 2020, and a few friends of ours invited us to go to Atlantic city with them. At first, I was very stubborn about not wanting to go but I was always one to say even if I don't want to go or do something, to make me do it because every time I actually do follow through on something I was hesitant with I end up realizing that I made the right decision. I had never been to Atlantic city before, so I realized why not get out and go have some fun and hang out with good people. We got dressed up and drove there and I was very impressed once we got there. They had swimming pulls and slot machines and several other things to do. I have never been one for playing with slot machines, but I was all for going for a swim. There was even a hot tub there and I thought that was a wondaful way to relax and unwind. I didn't realize there was going to be a pool and hot tub until we arrived. It was not a big issue as I could have always bought some swimming trunks there. We were going to have pizza for dinner and pizza has always been one of my favorite foods , I just do not like tomatoes sauce on my pizza but nowadays they can make pizza however you want it. I always had a lot of respect for our friend and her husband Annabelle and Eddie. Annabelle always has been so very loving whenever I was around. We all went up to the room and had a few slices of pizza and then we went out by the pool as we were going to have a few drinks. My partner Juan had himself a drink or two and then there was a girl that came up and started talking to us. She was being very friendly, touching our clothes and trying to take our shoes off. It seemed very odd the way she was touching us so much and Juan started touching her hair given that he was a hairdresser. I could not deny the fact that I was not jealous because I was. They started having conversations with each other in Spanish which was perfectly okay but I started to just get a weird feeling and it bothered me so much that I got pretty angry. Now I know I could be a over sensitive brat at times and I have made mistakes of my own but this feeling I was getting just became stronger and stronger that I freaked out and got angry. I didn't know if I was being paranoid or what. There was another girl that came to sit next to us and she seemed friendly at first. The girl that came to sit next to us was the girlfriend of the other girl that Juan was talking to in the pool whose hair he was also touching which really is not big deal when I thought about it. It was just the things they were talking about in Spanish that felt off to me. Sometimes you just have to trust your instincts. The girl that Juan was talking to in the pool name is Marianne and the girl who sat next to us who is her girlfriend is Alyssa. As Marianne and Juan continued to talk in Spanish as she tried to take his shoes and cloths off so he could get into the pull her girlfriend Alyssa whispered in me ear, "Do you know what he is staying about you? You should not had married him, He isn't the guy for you" She was warning me not to trust him" She was confirming suspicions that I had already in the marriage since practically it begin. There was a big part of me that felt like Juan was using me to get a green card. There were many times I tried to let it go and move on but then that feeling always came back especially whenever I was around him. The day Juan got his green card, something did not feel right again. I expected him to be incredibly happy that we would be able to have a life together but it was off because it appeared as though he was even more excited to have the card. I hadn't seen excitement like that in a while. It felt like the card was the most precious thing he could ever get in the world, it was extremely odd. It was like he did not even notice I was there as he called his friend and immediately screamed and shouted with joy "I GOT GREEN CARD!!!! YES!!!! I GOT GREEN CARD!!!! I GOT GREEN CARD!!! ITS MINE!!!! I GOT GREEN CARD!!! My instincts were telling me many times not to trust him because he was manipulating me and after Allyssa whispered in my ear that I should not trust him and that he is not the guy for me and to be careful I freaked out and he said we should just probably leave. As we were leaving Alyssa ran up and pushed him into a pool as everyone watched. Juan quickly got out of the pool threatening the girl as I stood between them both telling Juan that we had to leave because if the police came and he got into any trouble that it could cause him to be deported. We had to be married for 4 years for him to achieve full citizenship. As we were leaving Juan blamed me for Alyssa pushing him into the pool. Things were becoming coming confusing for me again as I did not understand how I could be responsible for him getting pushed into a pull. I drove us home and he gave me a lecture about how he was upset with me and I am responsible for what transpired that night and ghosted me as some kind of punishment.

CHAPTER 22

Something Does not feel Right Part 2

*A*ll relationships have their problems and I know there have been plenty of times that I was the toxic one and I am in no way ignoring that but the issues between us continued to rise as I continued to lose my grip on reality doubting everything that I knew. It was December and we were well on our way into the new year, and we got together with some friends of ours and went on to a luxurious ship which I thought was fantastic. Even though I was shy a lot of the time I enjoyed the time we got to hang out with great friends. The anxiety was beginning to take over again as I started to feel like I did not belong and my feelings started to get the best of me, so I became pretty upset because I knew I was never going to be able talk like Juan's friends. They all spoke so beautifully in Spanish, and I wished I could talk like them and maybe I would be able to fit in more. Some loved me just as I am, and I began to get the feeling that there were others I just could not click with. That's just how life is I realize now as you either vibe with someone or you do not and there is nothing wrong with that at all. Everyone was dancing so I said to myself screw it, take that leap and go up there and dance and it was amazing. We were all jamming to music, and everyone was having a blast, not to mention they had amazing food. A friend of ours and her husband loved to go on a luxury ship before the new year and they invited us. I began to feel a bit tipsy after drinking a bit of wine, but it was all worth it. Once the music came to a end we were all headed out there was still music playing outside and we all watched the fireworks, which were incredibly amazing. After the fireworks we all went back to the limo, and everyone was having a conversation with each other, and I looked at everyone and it just felt like they clicked so well, and I felt like an outsider in their group, and it was not their fault. It just felt like they were family in a way that I could not be with them, they all had a connection with each other, one that I would not be able to tap into. I began to let my feelings get the best of me yet again as I was being overly sensitive, and someone looked over at me asking if I was okay and out of the blue Juan shouted out to everyone in the Limo that I did not like them. Everyone in the Limo quickly became offended as that was not the case at all. I loved every one of them very much, the only problem was that I hated myself deeply because I could never fit into their circle. It had nothing to do with who they were in any way but when Juan told them that it was clear they had thought the worst of me. I quickly became even more upset because Juan shouted out that I hated who they were. Everyone looked at me and I just could not look back at them as it felt like they were starting to see me as monster now. I could not believe Juan would go so far as to have these wonderful people think I hate their culture. It was all a mistake; a misunderstanding and I did not know how I would ever explain to them that it was not true. I wouldn't want to blame Juan for anything, I guess you can say It was just a couple of unfortunate events. Once we arrived home Juan and I continued to argue, and he left the house and ghosted me for a few days. He would always ghost me for a few days or more and I always got the strange feeling that he enjoyed it why I was at home driving myself mad about the ways I acted like an overly sensitive child. One day Juan came home with this huge smug look on his face and went into the room. I kept my mouth shut for a while but then I said something to him, and he started holding up his cell phone and he was recording me, which was incredibly odd. As he was holding the phone recording me, I did start to yell at him, and he said he needed to record me because he needed proof. It was clear he was trying to show people that I was mentally unstable. I quickly grabbed the cell phone and ran as far as i could with it and he pushed me d own the stairs and he said look at the top of your head like it was my fault that I hit the wall. When I touched the top of my head I was bleeding badly. I became very angry, and I started to fight back until he left as I was going to call the police. After an intense argument and fight we just both wanted to be away from each other. I was beginning to feel like I could not trust anyone. There were times I started to think maybe he is right, maybe I am the bad one, maybe everything that has happened is my fault and yes there were times it was. I was beginning to feel like I had no one I could turn to so I turned to the one thing that I could ease the pain and that was drugs yet again. There were people who at the time I thought were actual friends and I started getting high with them and doing hard drugs again as I felt like a screw up that just could not do anything right or say the right thing. It was getting so bad for me that I started begging for forgiveness from him because I felt like the wrong one. I had gone from doing hardcore drugs occasionally, to just doing it practically every single day.

CHAPTER 23

Going back

*A*fter many ups and downs and feeling like Juan was playing mind games with me not to mention the fact that I could not tell right from wrong. It was time for me to divorce him so I went to file for divorce and blocked him so that there was no way he could text or call me. I could never blame anyone for me going back to drugs as that was my choice alone to make just like I could never blame anyone for me returning to drugs once again. I began hanging out with people that were once again a bad influence on me, but I did not care if I was getting high. What little friends I did have left I never wanted to see again, and I withdrew from family even on the holidays. Being used for a green card just sent me over the edge and I could not take it anymore. I posted an ad for a roommate that moved in with me for a while and I became paranoid even with him there. After a while he decided to move out and I continued to go and do drugs only this time I became so delusional thinking someone was targeting me that I took my frustration out on someone getting me into a lot of trouble with the police. I did not know what to believe anymore. The police concluded that I was mentally unstable and decided to take me to the hospital to get evaluated. As I was explaining to the hospital, it was clear they were going to admit me, and they did. I was strapped to a hospital bed kicking and screaming that they had to listen to me because I felt like I was being manipulated and used. It was such a horrifying experience as I felt like some kind of animal. I begged them to listen to me but all they could see was a crazy man who needed a lot of help and to an extent they were right. I tried to run out of the hospital only to be tackled by several guards and taken back to the hospital. They strapped my legs down to the hospital bed and they strapped my arms down and sedated me and I passed out only to wake up in another room with someone sitting next to me. The women stated that she was a nurse and that she was assigned to watch me. I felt like I had lost all control of my life, and I was starting to give up. No matter how hard I tried I could never truly give up as there was always that spark of light within willing me to keep going. The only thing that I knew no matter the circumstances was that I had to move forward no matter the circumstances, believing that one day I would have control of my life once again. After a week in the Hosptial I had been transported to a different mental hospital. My car had been towed to a shop nearby where the police had taken me into custody. In this new mental Hosptial I came across many other people who were also trying to heal and reclaim their life and some who had given up and just could not care. I felt every one of their pains. I had a police officer get in touch with my roommate so he could take care of my dog because I was in the hospital. There was a incredibly kind women that I met who was also staying at the hospital and we would always get together to watch movies around 8 or 8:30pm or we would watch the news in the morning. Her name was Nancy, and I knew instantly that she had such a wonderful. We would get together for counseling sessions and talk about certain events in my life. In a lot of ways Nancy and I inspired each other. I told her about people that I felt like were following me and that I thought it was Juan's friends attempting to start trouble and she surprisingly believed me. I stayed in the hospital for a few days and continued to get to know a few other people who felt comfortable enough to share their stories with me. A lot of people always came to me whenever they needed advice. I always had a way of inspiring people to greatness and one of my dreams was to make an impact in the world. After about a few days in the hospital, it was time for me to be discharged and I had to go get my car from the tow shop and I became determined to once again take my life back once more because giving up just was not in me no matter how bad things got. I had been there for so many others in their time of need and I owed it to myself to go forward but not carry the weight of my past. Our mistakes do not get to define who we are and no one us gets to define who we are so when times are hard it is important to remember that it is all part of the journey, and these are just our trials. I always knew who I was which was someone with such a loving heart and soul and I thank God for sending amazing people my way to remind me of that. There is an army of angels watching over me every single day. I know that I had to let go and let God and the universe guide me to where I needed to be.

CHAPTER 24

The universe and True Love

I continued to make poor choices with drugs and giving my trust to the wrong people on the verge of just completely giving up on life. There were friends and family that just wanted to make sure that I was okay, and I wanted nothing more but to crawl under a rock and hide from the world. You get to such a breaking point of wanting to know what is wrong with you, so I started doing some research about highly sensitive people and oh boy was I in for the shock of my life. My research led me to empaths which are individuals that can feel the emotions of others. It all started to make sense as to why people always called me crazy, or that I was so sensitive. I continued to do my research on empaths, and it just hit me that the universe had been trying to show me who I am for quite some time but when you're in so much pain you just want to hide from the world but sooner or later you must deal. The universe is never trying to punish us by teaching certain lessons. I know the universe has loved and supported me for as long as I could remember but it was time to let go and let God. As I discovered that I was a empath I noticed other things happening like certain people following me certain places, there were conversations that I was having with people that brought up Texas. I began scrolling through social media and I noticed a man who just seemed incredibly familiar like my soul recognized him instantly.

The man was in Dallas Texas. My heart and soul just felt drawn to him in a way that it never has with anyone else. You feel so drawn to someone and you do not know how to explain it. At first, I had thought maybe it was just a coincidence but there was something that kept drawing me back as if his soul was calling out to mine. As I would drive around to do my grocery shopping or go to work, I began noticing vehicles with actual Texas plates and more began to come together for me. This man was either in Dallas or Austin Texas of all places and I began to piece that the universe was leading me to him. I was driving home from work, and I noticed a car in front of me driving and it had Texas on the plate but this time it had Dallas written on the top as well confirming that this man who happened to be in Dallas and then another point happened to be in Austin. I knew that there was something in Austin and I knew that he was in Dallas, and it just became so much clearer that the two and he were connected. I knew that I had to work on myself, and the rest would continue to fall into place. It was time to make myself a priority and so the next phase of my healing journey. The universe was leading me to my one and only true soulmate and I was ready to listen and pay attention to the signs. There were people beginning to refer to me as the gifted chosen one and I began doing some more research as things were becoming clearer. The whole universe was supporting me, I just needed to not be so stubborn and take the walls down that I put up after being hurt many times by other people and that is not to ignore the fact that I hurt people too because of the pain that I had endured. I always knew that there was something different about me, reason why I could never really fit in with other people, wondering if there is one person out there who understood what it was like to be me and we always out there waiting for the day when I would return home to him. A coworker at work referred to me as the chosen one and said I was going to change the world not to mention that I would see many things in stores about other influential figures that have changed the world. I knew God had chosen me because of what he knew I could handle, because he knew that it would make me stronger and lead me to my destined path. As much as I knew my true love was out there, it was clear that I still had to care for myself as the priority because I still had some healing to do. I knew the other half of my soul was out there and no matter how hard the enemy would try to keep us apart that our love was stronger than anything that could be thrown at us. It was becoming more and more apparent that God needed the universe the universe to prepare me. Sure, there have been many times that I stumbled but by the grace of God I was determined to keep getting back up and going forward without the weight of my past or the weight of the world on my shoulders. Trusting the universe was a difficult process because when the universe is throwing everything at you, you can't help but wonder if it is because you are a terrible person or If the reason is because you are so loved and that is why it is so important for you to grow and change or actually both. A lot of my frustration and anger that I took out on other people was because I was not willing to listen at first but I knew that the only way was to trust where the universe was taking me no matter how disturbing things became because there is always purpose in our pain and that was key for the journey that I am on. It was time for me to take that quantum leap and although there were many times, I could still be stubborn, in my heart and soul I understood that my love was out there, and the universe was preparing me for the life I had so long desired. I knew this was my time the shine and I had gifts, a love and a light that needed to be shared with the world.

CHAPTER 25

A rebirth

s I was attempting to get my life back on track, I was beginning to feel more confident, and I felt like my old life was dying as a new one was beginning to emerge. I became bitter and even cruel because of all the terrible things that I went through in my old life, but it was time to put that all behind me. There were many people leaving messages on the bathroom walls that they were going to murder me, and my job just started to become more and more toxic every single day that I just could not deal with it anymore. I had been out of work for about a week due to not feeling well at all. In that week that i had been recuperating I began to think, what would the point be of going back as I knew I was meant for more and my job was not necessarily fulfilling anymore. I knew that I wanted to leave my job of working in the warehouse for some time. There was just too much drama at my job, it was almost like some people thrived off drama and it just was not the direction that I was headed in. I needed to be somewhere where I loved the work that I was doing and not having to settle for anything less. As I was headed back to work after recovering I walked inside my job and there was just this intense feeling that I was starting to get like it just was not where I was supposed to be so I told myself that it was no time like the present and I decided to take that risk and walk out and once I did that it was just clear that I made the right decision. Change can be very scary but absolutely worth it. Sometimes you just have to take that leap of faith and trust that everything will be okay. I think many of us want to be financially secure, but i t was time for me to not worry about that either. It was time for me to do what is best for me. As I left my job, I did call human resources once I returned home, and I told them I no longer wanted to work there because it was just too toxic, and I did not find the work fulfilling any more. OfCourse human resources wanted to ask me some more questions, but it just was no longer necessary as I knew that door had closed, and I was not going to let It open again. I thought maybe I could collect unemployment until I got a new job but that did not exactly work out. There were more signs that I was getting from the universe about becoming a caregiver so after a while it became clear that I could be of great help by taking a job as a home health aide. The universe was making it incredibly clear that was the path I should take so I just went for it. Helping people is what brings me joy so why not become a care giver. As I moved from Philadelphia to Lancaster to stay with friends and begin a new job, it really felt like my life was beginning to turn around. I had been hired to start my new job as a caregiver and I could not have been more thrilled as I was finally beginning to put the past behind me and starting a new chapter.

CHAPTER 26

Static energy Dots

As I was finally on the road to a fresh new start my psychic abilities started to manifest even more. I became unsure of what exactly was happening to me, and I knew that if I went to talk about it with anyone, they would most likely commit me to a mental institution, and I have never been a fan of hospitals, so I told someone that I worked with about what was happening. I needed to share what was happening with someone else that I could trust. The time came for me to finally tell my ex-coworker Kiki about what I had yet to understand. Kiki was always someone I could talk to about many different things that have developed in my life. I wanted to tell someone who has always been like a second mother to me, but it did not feel right talking about something like that on her phone as I have always trusted my second Mother Patricia more than anyone else, but I wanted to tell her the right way in person. I could see the psychic energy dots in the air outside, moving past windows and when I looked up and saw helicopters go by or airplanes, there were these wondrous orbs that were there moving right along with them. It was clear that God has blessed me with some amazing gifts. The energy dots and orbs were either beside people or attached to them in a way I could not yet fully understand. It was the most magical thing I had ever seen. I began to see auras around people as well. The more I seen the more I wanted to do my worship to confirm everything. It was clear the universe was leading me to this point on my journey and things began to make sense even more. There were conversations that I was having with people where it just felt like someone was tryng to get a message to me. There were the obvious messages certain individuals wanted me to have and then there were other messages where it felt like it was coming from the great beyond. It was like one of those movies or tv shows you watch and then you are certain one thing is being said and then you look back and the messages just seem deeper. Could I have been receiving messages from the other side? This led me to do some more research and I discovered some information about clairaudient which is the power to hear sounds said to exist beyond the reach of ordinary experience which are basically voices from the dead. I did not know how to fully make sense of it just that everything sounded different whether that was with sounds or words that came out of people's mouth or even television. Everything was beginning to shift for me and there were many times I over analyzed what was happening but that is why my research became so much helpful at putting things at Ease. I'm a big fan of True crime shows or anything where there is a huge mystery, and it is left up to the audience to put things together throughout the episode or movie. Being a good detective takes time, but it is something I enjoyed doing my whole life. Things were starting to come together in a big way why I never fit in with many others, why I always seemed so different from everyone yet so connected to everyone in such a big way that I could not explain. The universe has always supported me. I just needed to fall apart to come back together as my true self. Another psychic ability started to surface as well as I began seeing shadows go buy my eye. I noticed that everyone has a shadow. At first, I really overanalyzed the shadows, and some may laugh heavily today, and I would not blame them as I thought it was very funny myself, but I assumed they were dark spirits as I did not know what to make of it. I assumed it was the devil following people which I got wrong but hey I am human, so I look at all possibilities. The shadows going by my eye were not scary or frightening in any kind of way as I felt fascinated by them. I could also begin to see static energy within the light. Whenever I would sit in the living room with friends, I would see the white flashes above them or even appear next to pictures and sometimes next to my picture in my bedroom and I felt nothing but warmth inside when these lights appeared. As I woke up on a Saturday morning, I noticed tons and tons of white lights around me. It was the most magnificent thing I have ever seen. I felt safe and protected with these white lights like the spirits were letting me know that I am loved and that I am safe as the best is yet to come. I give so much credit to the universe for getting me on my path and for helping me see that is easy to lose faith in yourself sometimes but that is where you just have to let go and let God, so I thank the universe from the bottom of my heart for every blessing past, present and future as they helped restore me to my true self.

CHAPTER 27

A new path

For so long I never thought I would be able to find my way out of the darkness and fully step back into the light but somehow, I made my way back by the grace of God. It was time to forge my own unique path so I attempted to try several projects to feel what moves me heart and soul so I took online courses on how to write a book, signed up for programs where I could model and tried to sign up for acting workshops and I was already attending college part time and had my new job as a caregiver. Change can be scary but as scary as it can be it is so worth the risk. I would never want to look back wishing maybe I tried something new and then did not go for it as now is my time and I am ready to shine. The only way to achieve greatness is to take that leap of faith and trust that no matter what God will always take care of you. There were many times where I was nervous taking these risks but that is just is I think everyone gets nervous when trying something new, but I felt this new level of confidence that began to every day. I truly was beginning to feel like a new man. Even if I failed at something I was going to keep going until I found what it is that I loved in life, until I found my own identity. I went from people pleasing everyone to finally pleasing myself for once because in what better way can you show yourself some self-love than that? Life is far too short not to be happy and I was not about to throw my happiness away any longer. It was my time to soar to a new height. God has always seen me as unique; he sees all of us as unique but almighty God just wanted me to reach my true potential and let go and trust him and the magnificent universe to go forward without any fear of how things may go wrong. God saw a unique light in me and has given me amazing gifts to share with the world. He truly Is the light of my life. I do not think anyone can fully be healed from their past but if we can continue to learn from it then things truly will get better as everyone in this world is learning life lessons. Being psychic and seeing that seeing psychic energy and spirits as well as being a healer are gifts to be cherished and that is exactly what I was going to do. Even when I screamed and shouted at the universe, I knew deep down that it was not trying to hurt me but rather prepare me for the things that I have long waited for so long. Jesus has picked many flowers for my mom and I love imagining seeing the smile on her face when he says that they are from me just as I know she is smiling right now because she now that I am finally on the right path to greatness because that is exactly what I am destined for . There is nothing that we cannot overcome, and I am so proud of myself for how much I have overcome. My eyes are fully open now and it was time to shine my life, to shine it so bright that nothing will ever stop me again from living the life that I desire.

CHAPTER 28

Love

There are so many friends and family that have supported and loved me unconditionally over the years and I thank them from the bottom of my heart for always being there for me, especially through the dark time without judgement but words of encouragement. My mother's spirit will always be with me wherever I go, and I will also take her inspectional words with me wherever I go. To have a mother who loves you no matter what and wants to do everything in their power to make sure that you are happy and loved is a gift all on its own and she was not just a gift to me and our family but she was such a gift to the world and I find a great deal of comfort knowing that she is with the lord in the light. Jesus paid the ultimate price and died on the cross, paying for the sins of the world and I love him so very much because whatever I may be going through, I know Jesus is there waiting for me to talk to him. Adele, who is a gracious second mother, has been there for so long encouraging me to keep going and never give up because I am destined for greatness. No matter how far away we got from each other physically, I always felt her love. Whenever I called her, she always picked up and was there to talk to me and simply just listen first. I feel as though my mom made sure Adele always remained in my life because she wanted to make sure I had someone in my life I could turn to that would really understand me. There are my brothers Andre and Ronald who may not be perfect nor is anyone on this planet, but they are true warriors just as

I am. My brothers have conquered many obstacles in their life and even though we do not see each other every day, there is a bond between us, a connection that nothing can ever severe. Whether it is my chosen family or the family I was born into, I will forever love every one of them. Being given this opportunity to wright this book has just been so fulfilling to me and I thank Jane who has assisted me with my book because he is someone who is such a loving soul that would call to get updates about my book but would also take time out of his day to ask me how mine has gone and how school is and work is and more. New doors are opening for me and no matter if they ever close again, I know they will always open back up, possibly leading me towards bigger and better. My true love Is out there thinking of me every day just as I am thinking of him every single day. A love like ours is so powerful that nothing could ever break it. Loving myself is loving him because we share the same soul. Whenever I feel our love, it is like I I am flying in the sky as I know we are destined to be together. He has saved me over a countless number of times, and I know I have saved him many times as his light has touched my soul and mine has touched him. One day we will come together physically to begin the next stage of our journeys. He is in my dreams; he is in my heart and soul. He is forever my love, and I am forever his.

CHAPTER 29

Aliens

Growing up I have always been labeled as weird because of my fascination with aliens and believing there is other life out there in the world. I find it complementing being called weird and I would not have it any other way. Are we the ones with the alien DNA? I believe that could be quite possible, yet I still believe there is other life out there in the world on different planets. Are aliens good or evil? And if they are evil, why have they not come to attack us on earth. Could the aliens be witnessing all the chaos that is happening around the planet? The aliens could already be here, and we could have the alien DNA without most even realizing it. It's not like we always see in the movies or a tv show about an alien some of which are good and some of which want to take over the planet and claim it as their own. Sometimes I wish I could go in some type of ship into space with a device that could detect other life on other planets but then I also must consider what if I do go to the planets and this alien may not be so friendly. It Is all left up to speculation, but I will never stop looking and even if I find nothing then it comes back to my first conclusion that we are the aliens that have been here all along. Me being someone that is into true crime loves a mystery so I would have to investigate which I find to be very thrilling and find evidence to support my theory. Sometimes I even wonder if the aliens come to us when we are sleeping and do things to us causing us to wake up and then make it so that we do not remember anything in the morning.

Not only do I believe in aliens, I also have a love for the paranormal like when a spirit is nearby and I feel something on my arm which more like I can feel it on the hair on my arm or even my leg or when you get this intense feeling that someone is nearby because you could feel it. I can already see small white lights near people and objects and more so that is defiantly true. Growing up all the way up until the present day I have always been drawn to the paranormal like I have always had a foot in one world and another, not understanding why I am so different from everyone else but being different is what makes me special. As I watched many tv shows about the supernatural or even a chosen one I would act out a specific scene from what I was watching because I felt so drawn to it all. Sometimes you just must listen to your intuition and what my intuition was telling me is that I was always meant to stand out and that was something to never apologize for. Even if we human beings are the ones that are with alien DNA, I still believe there is another life out there and I fully intend on finding that life as I will never give up until the truth is discovered.

CHAPTER 30

Gratitude

My path has not always been easy, and I have not always made the best choices, but I am so grateful of where I am today because I am not stronger, and I am now wiser and I am finally in a place where I am not living in fear of going into the unknown. Not every day is going to be easy but through God I have found a peace within, and I know there is a light within me that needs to be shared with the world. My mother has prepared me, God has prepared me and used the universe to get me ready and for that I am forever grateful. There have been times where I felt like giving up but the lord's grace would will me to keep on going and that is exactly what I am going to keep on doing. My brothers have always been there for me whenever I needed them, and they are such wonderful blessings in my life. My mom was the most amazing gentle soul to ever grace this earth and she wll forever be carried in my heart and soul until one day we meet again but until then she will keep watching over me with God as they both continue to inspire me. Love is love and I want to share that love with the world even if some struggle to find that within their hearts. I am so grateful that God has forgiven me over and over because of my mistakes. We cannot change the past but we can learn from it and apply that to our present circumstances and be grateful because every day that we are still breathing is such a gift where as there are others out there in the world that are in a bad place just as I once was but we can continue to pray for them that one day things will get better. Sometimes you have to be the change that you hope to see in the world. Having faith can be a challenge especially when you feel like the universe is always throwing so much at you but what if they were tests to see how much you can handle. God sees in us what we sometimes do not always want to see in us, and we don't always see that we are destined for greatness because we are unwilling to listen. The path may not be easy, but it is so worth it. In the past I was manipulated and taken advantage of by many people but at the end of the day I made my own choices and I take full ownership of my actions. When you trust in God, nothing Is impossible so long as you keep on believing. To all that have supported me on this journey and even to the ones that may not have necessarily supported me I am still grateful because it all led me to this point of accepting me for me. There is no light without any darkness as it provides a perfect balance. I had to go through the bad to get to the good, I had to go through the darkness to find my way to the light. I am ready to soar to new heights and see what else is out there in the world. This is my time to show the world that I can handle anything that is thrown my way and I hope and pray that all my loved ones continue to be a part of my unique journey just as they always have. Thank you, God, from the bottom of my heart for always loving me and no matter where I go in this world, I know your light will continue shinning down upon on me as well as within.

CHAPTER 31

The light

So that is my story of how I had to face many trials in life, met some amazing people, faced some losses including myself at times and made my way from the darkness to the light. Life is such a journey that can be tough at times but when you keep going the end result is worth it and even if things do not always turn out exactly how you wanted it is still worth getting back up and trying again. It's not really living If you're not giving yourself the chance to be happy. I am finally in a place where I am willing to take that leap and trust that God will always provide for me just as he always has. Sure, there may be storms that we face at times, but every storm comes to an end eventually. The path may be hard at times but with love and patience you can survive anything the universe only has your best interest in mind. Letting go is hard but it is the only way you are going to be able to heal and you must heal those scars otherwise you never truly be free to live the life that you deserve. When they say there is a light at the end of the tunnel, there truly is so I would hope that anyone that is in any pain and feels as though they are alone in the darkness to rise up and make their way back into the light and fly high because there is always hope but you have to love yourself first, you have to value yourself first and when you do that you gain a confidence like you never thought possible. We are all unique and sure compliments are much appreciated but what matters the most is that we believe that ourselves. Doing what is right for yourself does not make you selfish at all. Never get to a place of thinking you wish you did something before when now the perfect time is to do it. Knowing that I have psychic abilities is such a wonderful gift as I feel like I am connected to two worlds now not to mention I am creative, imaginative and feel so connected to everyone and everything on the planet. The light is a part of me but what I had not known for some time is just how much a part of me that it was as things were beginning to feel and look different with the light whether I was outside or inside. I could be having a conversation with someone inside and I could feel the light change outside and look differently. All I knew was that something was incredibly different about the light and that it was connected to me. The light felt warm and peaceful. Every time I looked at the sun it was like there was someone watching me from up above and keeping me safe, it just started to feel like there was this presence in the light, and I could feel that presence. There are times I can overanalyze but knew in my heart and soul that I felt connected to the light as it was drawn to me. There were moments when the light responded when I was around certain people or in certain places as if someone was trying to communicate with me through the light. It felt like the light was telling me to be still, take a deep breath and relax because I am safe. So, the question then becomes If I am connected to the light, if the light is connected to me than what does that all mean? I guess I will have to save that story for the next book as the journey continues. This is my time, and I am going to share my light with the world, I am going to share my gifts that God has given me because I am Chosen!